Bizarre Beast Battles

CHEETAH VS. OSTRICH

Gareth Stevens
PUBLISHING

By Charlotte Herriott

Please visit our website, www.garethstevens.com. For a free color catalog of all our high-quality books, call toll free 1-800-542-2595 or fax 1-877-542-2596.

Library of Congress Cataloging-in-Publication Data

Herriott, Charlotte, author.
 Cheetah vs. ostrich / Charlotte Herriott.
    pages cm. — (Bizarre beast battles)
Includes bibliographical references and index.
ISBN 978-1-4824-2784-4 (pbk.)
ISBN 978-1-4824-2785-1 (6 pack)
ISBN 978-1-4824-2786-8 (library binding)
1. Cheetah—Juvenile literature. 2. Ostriches—Juvenile literature. 3. Animal behavior—Juvenile literature. 4. Animal weapons—Juvenile literature. I. Title. II. Title: Cheetah versus ostrich.
 QL737.C23H46 2016
 590.96—dc23
                                        2014048395

First Edition

Published in 2016 by
Gareth Stevens Publishing
111 East 14th Street, Suite 349
New York, NY 10003

Copyright © 2016 Gareth Stevens Publishing

Designer: Katelyn E. Reynolds
Editor: Therese Shea

Photo credits: Cover, p. 1 (cheetah) Fiona Ayerst/Shutterstock.com; cover, p. 1 (ostrich) rickyd/Shutterstock.com; cover, pp. 1–24 (background texture) Apostrophe/Shutterstock.com; pp. 4–21 (cheetah and ostrich icons) Voropaev Vasiliy/Shutterstock.com; p. 4 Eric Isselee/Shutterstock.com; pp. 5, 10 Bildagentur Zoobar GmbH/Shutterstock.com; p. 6 Anan Kaewkhammul/Shutterstock.com; p. 7 Dennis Jones/Lonely Planet Images/Getty Images; p. 8 Maros Bauer/Shutterstock.com; p. 9 paula french/Shutterstock.com; p. 11 Sergei25/Shutterstock.com; p. 12 Gallo Images - Heinrich can den Berg/Riser/Getty Images; p. 13 Villiers Steyn/Shutterstock.com; p. 14 Aron Ingi/Shutterstock.com; p. 15 iusubov/Shutterstock.com; p. 16 Maggy Meyer/Shutterstock.com; p. 17 Kip Ross/National Geographic/Getty Images; p. 18 Valdecasas/Shutterstock.com; p. 19 Persefoni Photo Images/Moment/Getty Images; p. 21 (cheetah) Lara Zanarini/Shutterstock.com; p. 21 (ostrich) Rafal Cichawa/Shutterstock.com.

Printed in the United States of America

CPSIA compliance information: Batch #CS15GS: For further information contact Gareth Stevens, New York, New York at 1-800-542-2595.

CONTENTS

Words in the glossary appear in **bold** type the first time they are used in the text.

SPOTTED SPEEDER

Cheetahs are known mostly for two of their famous features: A cheetah has black spots all over its yellowish body. It's also the fastest animal on land. This amazing ability makes cheetahs a frightening predator to many animals in their **habitat**, including birds, rabbits, gazelles, and antelope.

Almost all wild cheetahs live in Africa, but a small population is found in the **Middle East**. Only about 12,000 cheetahs remain in the wild today. They usually like to live alone—so they can keep their prey to themselves!

CHEETAHS HAVE "TEAR STRIPES," WHICH ARE BLACK MARKS THAT STRETCH FROM THE INNER CORNER OF EACH EYE TO THEIR MOUTH.

5

BIGGEST BIRD

The largest bird in the world can't fly. The ostrich has a small head, long neck, big body, and long legs. It doesn't have many feathers on its head or neck, and its strong legs are bare. Ostriches may not be able to fly, but they're superfast runners.

Ostriches are found in the open plains of Africa. They live in groups for **protection**, sometimes gathering in flocks of more than 100! Ostriches mostly eat plants, but also snack on small animals, such as lizards, **rodents**, and snakes.

OSTRICHES EAT SAND AND STONES, WHICH HELP BREAK DOWN THE FOOD THEY EAT.

7

FAST AND FASTER

Cheetahs and ostriches share habitats in Africa. Both can be found on grasslands looking for food. However, it's not common at all for these animals to interact. Can you imagine what would happen if they battled each other? The answer isn't as easy as you might think. Let's look at their top speeds.

 **NORMAL RUNNING SPEED:** 55 MILES (89 KM) PER HOUR

 TOP SPEED: 71 MILES (114 KM) PER HOUR

NORMAL RUNNING SPEED:
30 MILES (48 KM) PER HOUR

TOP SPEED:
45 MILES (72 KM) PER HOUR

The cheetah clearly wins this match. However, the ostrich can run a lot longer than the cheetah.

9

SIZING THEM UP

Cheetahs and ostriches definitely look different. After all, one is a cat and the other is a bird. However, it's still interesting to compare their sizes.

WEIGHT:
UP TO 120 POUNDS (54 KG)

LENGTH: 4 FEET (1.2 M) LONG, WITH TAIL UP TO 3 FEET (0.9 M) LONG

WEIGHT:
UP TO 330 POUNDS (150 KG)

HEIGHT:
UP TO 9 FEET (2.7 m) TALL

Both male ostriches and male cheetahs are a bit bigger than the females of their kind. Comparing these numbers, the ostrich definitely wins for height and weight. It's a good thing they only eat small animals!

WHAT A STRIDE!

Both animals can thank their amazing body and long **stride** for their remarkable swiftness. Both cheetahs and ostriches have **adaptations** that help them break speed records.

 SPEED ADAPTATION:
LONG TAIL FOR BALANCE

 SPEED ADAPTATION:
BENDABLE BODY TO CHANGE DIRECTION

 SPEED ADAPTATION:
STRIDE THAT COVERS UP TO 22 FEET (6.7 m)

SPEED ADAPTATION:
WINGS FOR BALANCE

SPEED ADAPTATION:
LONG LEGS

SPEED ADAPTATION:
STRIDE THAT COVERS UP TO 16 FEET (4.9 m)

Both animals could cross a room in your home with just one long step! However, the cheetah is the winner for stride length. A cheetah can complete about four strides per second.

13

EYEING THE ENEMY

Cheetahs have excellent eyesight. So, the big cat would easily be able to spot an ostrich from far away and speed toward it.

EYESIGHT:
EXCELLENT—CAN SEE ABOUT 3 MILES (5 KM) AWAY

14

EYESIGHT:
EXCELLENT—CAN SEE ABOUT 2 MILES (3.2 KM) AWAY

Ostriches can't see quite as far, but they still have great eyesight. They have the biggest eyeballs of any land animal! Part of the reason why ostriches live in groups is so that one bird is always looking out for danger. A cheetah might see the ostrich first, but the ostrich's friends might warn that the cheetah's coming!

15

BITE VS. KICK

Cheetahs are all about speed in everything they do. They chase prey at top speed and kill and eat it as quickly as possible. That's because they're afraid a bigger predator might steal their meal.

 ATTACK METHOD: KNOCK PREY TO GROUND

 ATTACK METHOD: KILL WITH BITE TO THE NECK

ATTACK METHOD:
KNEE BENDS LEG FORWARD

ATTACK METHOD:
POWERFUL KICKING FORCE TO STRIKE ENEMY

Ostriches don't really have to catch and attack their prey. But when they're cornered, they can deliver a terrible kick. How terrible is it? An ostrich's kick has been known to kill lions! Which sounds worse to you, the cheetah bite or the ostrich kick?

17

CLAW VS. TALON

Cheetahs have claws that don't **retract** all the way like house cats' claws do. This means their claws are always ready to grip the ground, which is another adaptation for high speed. They use their claws to hold down prey, too.

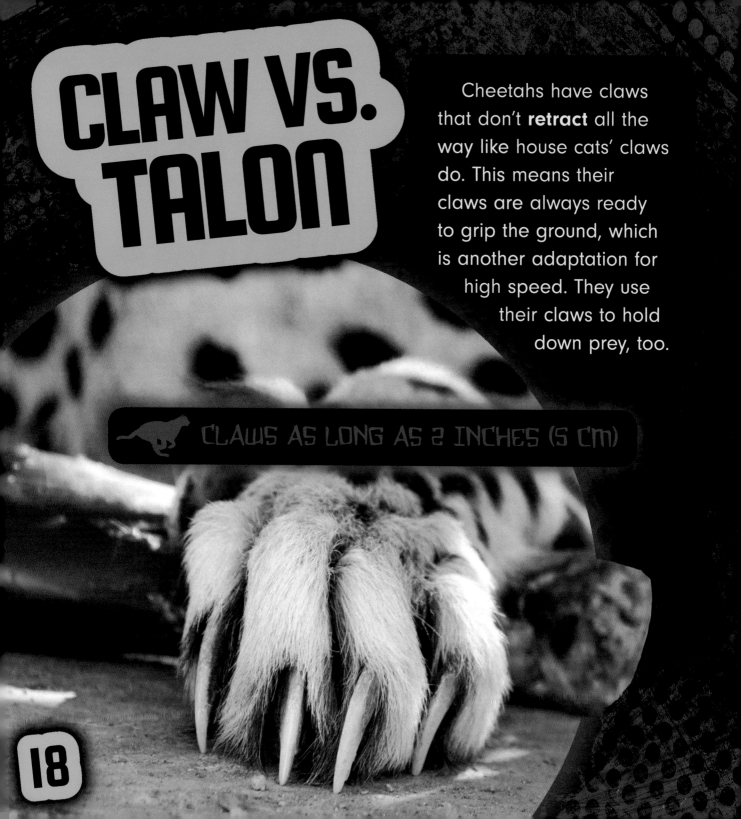

CLAWS AS LONG AS 2 INCHES (5 CM)

An ostrich is the only bird with two toes on each foot. Each foot has a **talon** that makes their deadly kick even worse. It can slice a body open! The cheetah's claws aren't very sharp. The ostrich's talons are definitely the more dangerous **weapon**.

THE WINNER?

Cheetahs and ostriches match up in other ways, too. For example, both can go long periods without drinking water, a handy adaptation in hot Africa.

So, if they were to fight to the death, which would win? A speeding cheetah could definitely catch an ostrich, but could the cat knock the bigger beast down and bite it? Would the big bird kick the cheetah with a deadly talon first? Use your imagination and the facts in this book to pick the winner of this bizarre beast battle!

 NOW THAT YOU KNOW MORE ABOUT THESE TWO AFRICAN CREATURES, YOU CAN DECIDE WHO'D WIN THIS MAKE-BELIEVE BATTLE.

21

GLOSSARY

adaptation: a change in a type of animal that makes it better able to live in its surroundings

habitat: the natural place where an animal or plant lives

Middle East: the area where southwestern Asia meets northeastern Africa

protection: the act of guarding

retract: to draw back or in

rodent: a small, furry animal with large front teeth, such as a mouse or rat

stride: a long step

talon: one of a bird's sharp claws

weapon: something used to fight an enemy

FOR MORE INFORMATION

BOOKS

Lunis, Natalie. *Ostrich: The World's Biggest Bird.* New York, NY: Bearport Publishing, 2007.

Silverman, Buffy. *Can You Tell a Cheetah from a Leopard?* Minneapolis, MN: Lerner, 2012.

Spilsbury, Louise. *Ostrich.* Chicago, IL: Heinemann Library, 2011.

WEBSITES

Cheetah
www.defenders.org/cheetah/basic-facts
Find out more about cheetahs and why there are so few in the wild.

Ostrich
animals.sandiegozoo.org/animals/ostrich
Read many more fun facts about ostriches.

INDEX